OUR LADY OF LORETO'S VICTORY

Our Lady of Loreto's Victory

THE BATTLE OF LEPANTO
SCREENPLAY

Dr. ant

Anthony T Vento

Saint Norbert Media, Inc

Contents

1

DRAFT 001

<u>BATTLE OF LEPANTO SCREENPLAY</u>

Written by

Dr. ant

BLACK SCREEN

Sound of warhorses, battle cries, trumpets, and cannon fire are punctuated by the rhythmic staccato of kettle drums.

Explosions thunder, the sound of rocks tearing away from each other follow.

WHITE TEXT ON BLACK

ACRE - KINGDOM OF JERUSALEM - 1291

EXT. ACRE - KINGDOM OF JERUSALEM - DAY

A large seaside city, surrounded by double stone walls. Inside the interior wall stands a formidable tower.

A sea of red clad soldiers besiege the walls with fire arrows. Trebuchets launch large loaded cloths that are lit and explode inside the city.

The wall leans and lists, beginning to crumble in places.

Near the tower, a phalanx of red clad soldiers make a directed attack on the wall and its defenses. They inch closer to the tower with each wave.

Arrows fly down from the tower, raining on the attackers. The attackers defend with shields.

Between each wave of arrows, the attackers gain ground.

EXT. ACRE - DAY

Stretching to the horizon behind the walls and the city it protects the vast expanse of the Mediterranean sea.

Wooden ships are hove to some distance offshore, sails furled and oars still.

Smaller boats navigate the coastal waters back and forth between the shore and the waiting ships. Aboard the small boats, oarsmen ferry women and children out to the larger ships as the city burn behind them.

THIBAUD GAUDIN, harried, sword at his side, rushes a WOMAN and two SMALL CHILDREN, a boy and a girl, through the panicked crowd towards the sea.

He crashes through soldiers and civilians alike.

The boy at his side stumbles and falls. The rush of the crowd threatens to crush him.

Thibaud crashes into the oncoming rush to divert them around the boy. He picks him up and carries him in his arms. The woman and girl have gained ground ahead of them.

EXT. SEASIDE - DAY

The woman and girl rush up to the sea and wade into the surf. Thibaud and the boy come shortly after them, and the four of them stand shin deep, deeper still for the children, in the water.

A small boat with a grizzled OARSMAN pulls along side and reaches for the girl's hand. She turns and clings to the Thibaud.

GIRL Papa, no!

THIBAUD

You have to go now, baby. Mama will be with you.

BOY

Where will you be?

THIBAUD

I will be where God has called me.

Thibaud picks her up and places her in the boat. The woman places the boy in next to her.

Thibaud and the woman embrace.

OARSMAN

We have to go! Now!

Thibaud and the woman pull apart. She hesitates. He embraces her again.

THIBAUD

Trust in God. He will carry you.

And explosion rocks the air. They turn to see:

THE TOWER COLLAPSES.

The woman lets out a gasp. Thibaud crosses himself.

OARSMAN

They'll breach any moment! I cannot wait any longer!

Thibaud helps the woman into the boat. She reaches for the girl.

The children look to their father, terror visible through their tears. He kisses them both, then the woman.

He taps the side of the boat, and the oarsman pulls away towards the waiting ships.

Thibaud crosses himself.

THIBAUD

May God be with you, my loves.

Thibaud watches them row out to sea. A tear falls. Then another. He is about to fall apart when -

A rushing, rumbling sound trembles through the air. Thibaud turns to see:

THE INNER WALL OF THE CITY COLLAPSES.

He charges towards the city as red clad soldiers rush through the massive breach.

EXT. TEMPLAR FORTRESS - DAY

A massive fortress stands sentry over the expanding destruction. Thibaud stands at the gate, rushing men, women, and children inside.

THIBAUD Hurry! Hurry!

Another explosion rocks the city.

The rest of the wall collapses.

The last few stragglers stumble their way over fallen bodies and into the fortress gate.

Thibaud takes one last glance around, then rushes inside and slams the gate firm.

INT. TEMPLAR FORTRESS - NIGHT

Thibaud stands looking out a window, down on the rubble of the city.

Bodies litter the ground.

The earth is red with blood.

Ottoman soldiers surround the castle.

Fires burn in an ordered pattern, illuminating the red clad Ottomans. In the glow of the fire their uniforms are the color of their victims' blood.

A door opens behind him. He turns to see a STOOPED MAN, wearing a Templar cross.

MAN

They are here. We must go now.

Thibaud nods and follows him out.

INT. LIBRARY - NIGHT

Thibaud and the man enter the fortress library. Books and parchments line the walls.

Next to one of the shelves are three large crates, each secured with intricate locks.

THIBAUD This is all?

MAN

All that remains, yes.

THIBAUD

Then we should go while God gives us grace to do so.

The man reaches between two of the bookcases. A click. He slides the bookcase aside to reveal a small passageway.

Moonlight sneaks in to illuminate stone walls leading out of the fortress.

They move the crates into the passageway.

INT. PASSAGEWAY - NIGHT

Thibaud slides the hidden wall back in place. He gives it a final nudge until there is a click.

He nods to the other man and they start moving the crates down the corridor.

EXT. TEMPLAR FORTRESS - NIGHT

Thibaud and the man drag the crates out of the passageway into the sound of the surf.

A bay sits calm before them. On the shore, two small boats sit waiting, oarsmen standing by.

Out at sea, barely visible in the dark of a moonless night, is a small galley ship.

The oarsmen help Thibaud and the man list the crates into the small boats, then they all row out towards the waiting galley.

BLACK SCREEN

WHITE TEXT:

The fall of Acre in 1291 marked the end of the crusades in the Levant, and was the last major stronghold in the Crusader Kingdom of Jerusalem to fall.

Under cover of darkness, the Templar treasure was smuggled out of the Templar fortress and taken to Sidon.

Eighteen days later, a peace was negotiated between the remaining Templars and the Ottomans. Aside from a few deaths, the peace accord was honored.

INT. APOSTOLIC PALACE - DAY

SUPER: APOSTOLIC PALACE, ROME, 1571

Filtered sunlight shimmers through stained glass to illuminate an otherwise dark room with shifting shadow and light.

The light reveals reredos and walls covered with frescoes of scenes from the life of Christ that extend up to and across the ceiling above.

Triptychs of Gospel scenes hang lower, creating a layered effect so as one starts from the bottom they follow the life of Christ from birth up the frescoes into the crucifixion, then to the ascension and subsequent revealed glory in the stained glass.

On the back wall hangs a large crucifix. A nailed Jesus looks down beneath a crown of thorns at POPE PIUS V, 60s, bald, full white beard.

Pope Pius kneels before the crucifix in a white, hooded robe, with the hood flipped back behind him. His hands clutch a cross hanging from his neck by a gold chord. His lips move, almost imperceptibly, in silent prayer.

A robed cleric appears in the shadows, almost blending in with the shifting darkness.

Shafts of colored light from the stained glass make the figure appear almost an illusion, shifting in and out of the shadows.

The figure stands a moment, then moves to the side of the room.

The figure lights a candle. The light from the candle reveals the worried face of CARDINAL ANTONIO CARAFA, 30s, well-kept dark beard. He wears a red cassock and red mozzeta and stands in the light of the candle for a moment, watching Pope Pius.

Pope Pius does not turn around.

POPE PIUS V Light the rest.

Carafa pauses, then takes the candle around the room, lighting the remaining candles.

As the candles are lit, the light in the room brightens to a soft glow, mixed with the hues of the stained glass.

The frescoes become clear.

Carved reliefs stand out from walls in the corners of the room.

Pope Pius takes a seat in a chair and regards Carafa.

POPE PIUS V (CONT'D)

You have something on your heart.

CARAFA

The Turks, your holiness.

POPE PIUS V

I am aware of the Turks.

CARAFA

Their ships are moving towards Cyprus. Our intelligence suggests they will attack Famagusta within weeks.

Pope Pius takes this in. Looks to the crucifix. Fidgets with his cross.

POPE PIUS V I thought

as much.

CARAFA Your holi-

ness?

POPE PIUS V My spirit has been burdened of late. I didn't know where they would attack, but somehow our Lord has made me aware that they were coming.

CARAFA

And does our Lord intend to send help?

POPE PIUS V

Yes, and I intend to gather it. It is time for a new Holy League.

CARAFA

Your Holiness, a Holy League has never -

POPE PIUS V

I am aware of the risks, Cardinal. And I am aware of the history. I am also aware of the Spirit's guidance.

CARAFA

If the Lord wishes to defeat the Turks, why would he insist on a new Holy League? Why not send a storm and drown them at sea?

POPE PIUS V

If the Lord wanted to part the Red Sea, why not just part it? Why make Moses hold his staff over the waters?

CARAFA

This is not the same.

POPE PIUS V

It is the same. It is always the same. When was Naaman cured of his leprosy?

CARAFA When he bathed seven times in the Jordan.

POPE PIUS V At whose behest?

CARAFA The prophet Elisha.

POPE PIUS V And on whose authority did Elisha speak?

CARAFA On God's authority, of course.

POPE PIUS V And did Naaman wish to do God's will when he heard it?

CARAFA No.

POPE PIUS V Was it God's will for Naaman to be healed?

CARAFA I ... I would venture yes, your Holiness. Otherwise he would not have healed him.

POPE PIUS V Yet still, the Lord did not heal Naaman until Naaman obeyed. Until he took action. Until he did the thing he did not want to do.

CARAFA And a new Holy League is our Jordan?

POPE PIUS V God has revealed his will, Cardinal Carafa. And, in his infinite grace and mystery, has made us the instruments of that will.

CARAFA Yes, of course.

POPE PIUS V Send my secretary. I will dispatch letters forthwith.

INT. PALACE OF KING PHILIP II OF SPAIN - NIGHT

Revelers dance in formal attire. WOMEN spin in billowing dresses, MEN spin them in their formal pantaloons.

The spinning whirls to the rhythm of a small chamber orchestra, playing from an elevated platform near the far wall.

A buffet of delicacies is set out, and servants bring food and drink around the room.

Near the buffet, holding a glass of wine, and holding court over a group of ENTHRALLED guests, is DON JUAN OF AUSTRIA, early 20s, dashing, smile like the sun, King Philip II's half brother.

Among the guests surrounding him is MARIA, 20s, beautiful, touching Don Juan's arm every time she laughs at one of his comments.

DON JUAN

To this day Granada wonders how it will get along without me.

The group laughs. Maria touches his arm. Don Juan beams.

MARIA

As do I, Don Juan.

DON JUAN

Ah, Maria. May you never have to do so.

MARIA

I have done so thus far.

DON JUAN

Perhaps today is our lucky day.

Maria touches his arm again. This time the touch lingers.

MARIA Perhaps.

EXT. PALACE OF KING PHILIP II OF SPAIN - NIGHT

GUARDS stand sentry outside as a foggy mist settles in over the palace.

The sound of the revelers can be heard drifting out of the windows and into the creeping fog.

A sound of hoofbeats alerts the guards. They focus their trained eyes on the direction of the sound.

From out of the fog a RIDER appears, illuminated by speckled moonlight. He stops his horse and dismounts twenty feet from the guards, who regard him with cautious eyes. Hands rest on sword hilts.

The rider approaches one of the guards and produces a letter. The guard looks at the seal. It is the seal of Pope Pius IV.

RIDER

For his excellency, the king.

He bows and returns to his horse. Mounts and rides away.

The guard watches him go, glances down at the letter. Walks into the palace.

INT. PALACE OF KING PHILIP II OF SPAIN - NIGHT

Don Juan is now alone with Maria. They are standing quite close.

DON JUAN

And how is it that I find myself alone with such a lovely

woman?

MARIA

It is your good luck, I think.

DON JUAN

We shall see which of us is the lucky one.

MARIA

Perhaps we are both lucky.

Don Juan smiles and starts to say something. He is interrupted by a blast of trumpet from the far side of the room.

The crowd quiets and stills. From behind an arched doorway appears KING PHILIP II, 30s, handsome in his royal attire.

All bow. King Philip waves a dismissive hand.

> PHILIP
>
> Please. Do not let me spoil the evening. Continue with the music and fun.

The chamber orchestra begins again. The revelers cheer and resume their dances.

King Philip makes his way through the crowd, stopping to chat with people here and there. People bow as he passes.

He approaches Don Juan and Maria.

> MARIA
>
> Your majesty. What an honor to be in your company.

> PHILIP
>
> I fear I may be distracting you from the honor of my brother's company.

> DON JUAN I fear this, as well.

Philip and Don Juan exchange a smile.

> PHILIP
>
> When have I ever shown a desire to restrict your proclivities, Don Juan?

> DON JUAN
>
> Only every time I see you.

Philip turns to Maria.

> PHILIP
>
> I'm afraid my brother is right. And I'm afraid I have need of him at the moment.

> MARIA
>
> And if I have need of him? What then?

> PHILIP
>
> Some needs are better savored after postponement.

> MARIA
>
> So long as he is not postponed too long.

> DON JUAN
>
> I assure you, Maria. I will return as soon as my brother releases me.

> MARIA
>
> After which you will be mine until I release you.

> DON JUAN

A pleasant thought to keep my heart warm in the mean-
time. (to Philip)

Very well, then. How may I assist you, your majesty?

King Philip gestures for Don Juan to follow him.

Maria watches them walk back through the crowd and disappear through the arched doorway.

ROYAL OFFICE OF KING PHILIP II - NIGHT

Philip stands looking out a large window at the mist and fog. Moonlight reflect in the mist, creating a glow that hovers over the grounds.

Don Juan stands nearby, reading the letter that was delivered earlier.

DON JUAN

A new Holy League? Has he lost his mind?

Philip whirls on him, snatches the letter away.

PHILIP

Careful how you speak of His Holiness.

DON JUAN

I mean no disrespect. But who can be trusted? The French? They are merely turks under another name.

PHILIP

Venice, perhaps.

DON JUAN

Please. They have more trade with the Turks than with us.

PHILIP

I do not know, Don Juan. But His Holiness would not undertake this without prayer.

DON JUAN He will
need it.

PHILIP

We will all need it.

DON JUAN

So you are considering this?

Philip pauses. Walks back to the window. Looks out over the estate.

PHILIP

We need to increase our revenues. If we can form a Holy League, we can charge for our ships and our soldiers.

DON JUAN

Now I see. Not just for God. For God and profit.

PHILIP

The kingdom is fragile, Don Juan. All of Europe is fragile.

DON JUAN And you expect it to be
strengthened by our banding against a common enemy?

PHILIP

Is that so insane?

DON JUAN

Yes. It is. Much of Europe already trades with the Turks. They won't risk that money for the Pope. Not even for God.

PHILIP But will they risk their independence for the Turks money? Most of Europe is now in the pocket of one Turk or another.

(MORE)

PHILIP (CONT'D)

Trade deals keep the money flowing. But what happens when the Turks decide they want more? More product? More land? France may give their people up to save the king, but Spain will not. I will not.

DON JUAN

You will be fighting alone. Venice won't join, or if they do they will have one foot on our side and one on the side of the Turks.

PHILIP

The Papacy is in. Genoa will join. Malta will join.

DON JUAN Malta? Malta can barely defend Malta.

PHILIP

Be that as it may. We will not be fighting alone.

DON JUAN You will be outnumbered by thousands. And half the troops you have will have their loyalties divided.

PHILIP

Yes. Yet there is one ally you have not counted on. God himself will sail with us.

DON JUAN

I wish I had your faith, brother.

PHILIP

Until you do, I will strive to have enough for both of us. We leave for Rome tomorrow.

DON JUAN

We? Why must I be there?

Philip gives him a long look.

PHILIP

I wish I knew. I just have ... a feeling.

DON JUAN

But -

PHILIP Tomorrow.

INT. VATICAN - DAY

Servants adorn a long table with golden bowls of fruits and berries. The produce glistens in the sunlight that streams in through wide windows.

Along the back wall scribes sit at small tables. Each table has a quill feather pen, a bottle of ink, and paper.

The scribes are dressed in understated vestments.

The door opens and the servants setting the table quickly finish and scurry out.

The scribes stand.

A man enters, somewhat more formally dressed than the servants who set the table. He stops inside the door and stands to the side.

He raises a paper and reads each name in turn.

ANNOUNCER

Paolo Giustiniani Moneglia, Doge of Genoa.

Swaggering into the room is PAOLO GIUSTINIANI MONEGLIA, Doge of Genoa, hook nose and sharp chin accentuated by a full brown beard. He wears a royal robe and crown of felt.

Behind him is a the SECRETARY OF GENOA. He enters, head down, almost shrinking into the room.

Moneglia takes a position at the table and stands. His secretary crosses to stand by one of the unoccupied desks.

ANNOUNCER (CONT'D)

Alvise I Mocenigo, Doge of Venice.

A light stepping ALVISE I MOCENIGO, 40s, soft eyes and a long, full beard, enters wearing a robe less formal than Moneglia, yet somehow he seems even more regal.

With him is a the SECRETARY OF VENICE, who takes a position by one of the empty desks.

Mocenigo walks to the table and stands behind a chair next to Moneglia.

ANNOUNCER (CONT'D) King Philip

II of Spain.

Philip enters, regal but modest. Don Juan comes in behind him, less regal and less modest. He swaggers as he follows his brother, head high.

Philip crosses to the table to stand next to Mocenigo. Don Juan comes with him.

Philip gives Don Juan a shrinking look. Don Juan shrugs. *What?*

Philip sighs and gestures towards the desks in the back. Don Juan looks at them, then glares at Philip. *Are you kidding me?*

Philip makes an urgent but understated gesture towards the desks. Don Juan hesitates. Sighs. Shakes his head. Walks over and stands next to an empty desks. Glares.

ANNOUNCER (CONT'D) Pietro de

Monte, Grand Master of the Knights of Malta and the

Order of Saint John.

Enter PIETRO DE MONTE. Sharp nose, hard eyes, battle hardened expression. Carries the memories of hard fought battles in his gate.

He does not bring a secretary. He takes his place by the table next to Philip. Philip nods a greeting. Pietro gives an almost imperceptible bow of the head and a slight smile.

ANNOUNCER (CONT'D) Cosimo I de'

Medici, Grand Duke of Tuscany.

Enter COSIMO I de' MEDICI, Grand Duke of Tuscany. Younger than the others, closer in age to Don Juan. Confident eyes and a walk that demands others to step aside.

Behind him is the SECRETARY OF TUSCANY, older, 50s, tired eyes and a silent walk that is almost a glide.

The secretary takes his place at an empty desk next to the still glaring Don Juan. Cosimo takes his stand by the table next to de Monte. He is slightly shorter than the others, but somehow looks taller in his confidence.

ANNOUNCER (CONT'D)

Emmanuel Philibert, Duke of Savoy.

Stepping in the room with a mix of military bearing and grace, EMMANUEL PHILIBERT, Duke of Savoy, is a sight to behold. 40s, well trimmed beard, eyes that have seen death one too many times. Only his head is visible above his exuberant attire.

Behind him is the officious SECRETARY OF SAVOY, sharp face and the bureaucratic bearing. He marches to the desks and stands by an empty one. He looks at the other secretaries and smirks.

Philibert takes his place next to the table, standing by Cosimo. He plucks a strawberry from one of the bowls and tosses it into his mouth.

ANNOUNCER (CONT'D) Guidobaldo II

della Rovere, Duke of Urbino.

GUIDOBALDO II della ROVERE, Duke of Urbino, jet black hair blending seamlessly into a full beard, steps into the room. He is dressed more for leading a military campaign than negotiating a new Holy League.

The SECRETARY OF URBINO follows, scurrying to take his place at one of the empty desks.

Rovere moves to the table and stands next to Philibert.

ANNOUNCER (CONT'D)

Ottavio Farnese, Duke of Parma.

Sliding into the room is OTTAVIO FARNESE, Duke of Parma. Long face, receding hairline, thin beard topped with a full mustache. He wears a black formal robe with a white collar.

Behind him enters a woman, MARGARET OF PARMA, stern expression, cold eyes, wearing regalia much more formal than the Duke.

Ottavio goes to the table and takes a place next to Rovere. Margaret follows him. Murmurs fill the room.

Ottavio glances at Margaret and shakes his head. Gestures towards the tables in the back.

MARGARET

I will not be reduced to your servant, Ottavio.

More murmurs. Whispers. Ottavio fidgets.

OTTAVIO

Margaret, please. It is not done. Not here.

MARGARET

If not here then where?

Don Juan steps forward. Smiles that charming smile. Bows to Margaret.

DON JUAN

Madame, please. I am the brother of King Philip of Spain,
and heir to half the kingdom. But even my status is not such
that I may sit at the table.

MARGARET

Your status is one of hierarchy. Mine is of gender. It is not
the same manner of disrespect.

DON JUAN

There is no disrespect intended, Madame. Long tradition dic-
tates the rules of order.

MARGARET

Perhaps it is time for tradition to die.

DON JUAN

Perhaps one day. But today we must defend ourselves
against an enemy far stronger than tradition.

Margaret glances back at the table. Looks at Ottavio. He gives her a pleading look.

MARGARET

And as a woman, I am relegated to stand and watch as men
make the world?

Don Juan bows again.

DON JUAN

Not at all, Madame. But perhaps while these men quibble
over contracts, you might enjoy the company of a man who
is heir to half of Spain, and who would be honored to have
you in his presence.

Margaret smiles. Ottavio bristles.

Margaret bows to Don Juan.

MARGARET

Perhaps there are better ways to occupy myself than with
the middling affairs of feeble men.

She walks with Don Juan to the back tables and takes the one next to his.

An uneasy relief settles over the room.

The announcer clears his throat.

ANNOUNCER

His Holiness, Pope Pius IV.

Pope Pius enters, wearing vestments suited to the occasion. He crosses the room to a small altar
above which hangs a crucifix. He kneels. The rest of the room kneels.

POPE PIUS V

Almighty and most merciful God, the one creator of all
that is created, the giver and sustainer of life, we ask that your
hand would be upon us, and that your spirit would guide us
to conduct your business with all wisdom and discernment.
Be present with us, Oh Lord, to guide and direct, that we
might walk in your light and delight in your will. We beg
your mercy and grace in the name of your son and our Lord
Jesus Christ, who lives and reigns with you and the Holy
Spirit, one God, now and Forever, amen.

Pope stands and faces the room.

The others stand. Pope Pius surveys them for a moment, as if wondering what God could
possibly do with this group of tenuous allies.

POPE PIUS V (CONT'D) Please, sit.

Everyone takes their seats. The royalty at the table, the others at the desks along the back wall.
Pope Pius takes his seat at the head of the table.

POPE PIUS V (CONT'D) I propose we
begin by taking inventory of what each of you can commit
in terms of ships, supplies, and personnel.

ROVERE

This is ridiculous. Contribute to what? We haven't even
agreed to band together.
                    DE MONTE
If you don't wish to band with us, why are you here?
                    MOCENIGO
He is here to see how much money he can make. If the Turks
offer more he'll band with them.
                    ROVERE
You are one to talk! Venice has one foot in the Turkish sands,
and the other in their banks.
                    MOCENIGO
Venice is here to win.
                    ROVERE
To win profits at the expense of the rest of us.
Mocenigo leaps from his chair. Rovere stands, challenging him.
All the others, except Pope Pius, stand as if a battle is about to be fought across the table.
Don Juan shakes his head and leans over to Margaret.
                    DON JUAN Here we go.
Pope Pius holds up a hand.

POPE PIUS V

            Gentlemen, please. Sit.
Tension hangs across the table. Mocenigo sits, glaring at Rovere. Rovere sits, straight as a flag
in a stiff wind.
After a moment, the others sit.
                    POPE PIUS V (CONT'D) If we are not in
            agreement on being in agreement, then perhaps we should
            start there.
INT. VATICAN - DAY
Much later. Even the royalty slouch and slump. Exhaustion fills the room. Pope Pius maintains
his composure.
                    MONEGLIA
If Spain wants to provide the ships, then let them.
                    PHILBERT
And Genoa provides nothing?
                    MONEGLIA
We will provide what is required, but it seems to me that
Spain is trying to commandeer the entire fleet.
                    PHILIP

We are commandeering nothing. We will provide ships.
Genoa is welcome to provide them as well. Venice has a
shipyard, they are welcome to add to the fleet. But as of yet
no one else has offered.

DE MEDICI

We cannot have ships from hither and yon. We need a
unified fleet. Not one separated among governments.

POPE PIUS V

It will be unified. Under the Holy
League. One fleet. One military. Under God's command.

FARNESE

My apologies, Your Holiness. But how is that to be? Will
you sail as admiral?

POPE PIUS V

The league will select a man fit to be admiral, and he will
lead the fleet.

MONEGLIA

I have difficulty believing that a man from one country can
command a fleet built from many.

POPE PIUS V

Have faith in God, Doge.

FARNESE

Faith in God is one thing. But the sailors will have to have faith
in their admiral.

DE MEDICI

Not necessarily. The sailors will need to have faith in their
respective captains. That will be simple. It is the captains who
must have faith in the admiral.

MONEGLIA

And who among us would be trusted by all?

PHILIP

Not among us, but with us.

All eyes turn to Philip. He gestures towards the back of the room.

PHILIP (CONT'D)

My brother. Don Juan of Austria.

Don Juan's eyes go wide. Seriously?

Margaret smiles.

MONEGLIA So we are back
to Spain commandeering the fleet!

MOCENIGO

I think this is a good idea. Who better to lead our fleet than
a man so young and inexperienced that he won't have the sense
to be afraid when he should?

Don Juan stands.

DON JUAN

Are you challenging my ability to lead?

MOCENIGO

Quite the opposite. If we are looking for a man of faith, we
need one who will charge ahead when God calls, and not be
held back by the fear born of hard experience. You are a man
of faith, are you not?

A beat. All eyes on Don Juan. He bristles, but keeps his cool. Smiles, even.

DON JUAN

If I was not, would my brother trust me with this?

POPE PIUS V

You are willing to do this, Don Juan, not for your own
glory, but for the glory of God?

Don Juan hesitates. Then stands tall.

DON JUAN

Yes, your Holiness. I will do this for God.

He looks at Philip. Philip smiles.

DON JUAN (CONT'D) For God and
profit.

A beat. The entire room erupts into laughter. Even Pope Pius gets a chuckle.

DE MEDICI

Spoken like a true Spaniard!

EXT. VATICAN - DAY

Don Juan stands tall amidst the buildings of the Vatican.

Margaret stands with him, an admiring smile as they talk.

MARGARET

I suppose I should call you Admiral now.

DON JUAN

A woman as lovely as you may call me anything you like.

Margaret smiles brighter. Laughs.

MARGARET

Careful, Admiral, or my husband will think you're coming for Parma next.

DON JUAN

I have enough to keep me busy outside of Parma. But if I happen to be in town …

MARGARET

You will be welcomed to dinner with me. And my husband.

DON JUAN

I would have it no other way.

Behind them, Philip and Ottavio approach. Ottavio glares.

OTTAVIO

Margaret. We need to be going.

Margaret bows to Don Juan.

MARGARET

It was a pleasure speaking with you, Admiral.

Don Juan bows in turn.

DON JUAN

Your servant, Madame.

Margaret walks to a glaring Ottavio and takes his arm. They walk away as Philip comes to stand next to his brother.

PHILIP

Ottavio is a jealous man, Don Juan. Take care that you remain alive long enough to lead the fleet.

DON JUAN

I can't help it if a woman wants to congratulate me on my new position.

PHILIP

Yes, it seems congratulations are in order.

DON JUAN

No. Thanks are in order. Thank you for doing this. Thank you for trusting me.

PHILIP

I need you there. I need someone I can trust. The economic risks to us are too great.

DON JUAN

I understand. I will not let you down.

Philip puts a hand on his shoulder.

PHILIP

Above all, Don Juan, do this for God.

DON JUAN

Of course. For God. And profit.

Philip smiles and pats his shoulder.

PHILIP

Tomorrow we select your second in command. I will let

you know what we decide.

He walks off. Don Juan stands in the middle of the grounds, lit by the setting sun, watching him go.

INT. PUB - NIGHT

A pub in Rome. Drinks are had. Tales are told. Laughs echo throughout.

Don Juan sits alone at a table in the corner, watching the revelers. A mug of ale rests in his hands.

Another mug drops on the table in front of him. And dropping into the chair opposite is Pietro de Monte.

They look at each other for a long time.

Finally:

DE MONTE

You will either lead us to victory

or lead us to death.

DON JUAN That could be said of anyone.

Those are the only two options.

DE MONTE

I am pleased to hear you say it. At least I can sleep knowing

you are aware of the stakes.

He spins his mug of ale slowly on the table.

DON JUAN

I have seen battle, Grand Master.

DE MONTE Not like

this.

DON JUAN

Then I will be pleased to hear your council.

DE MONTE

My council is to pray.

DON JUAN

Prayer is not a military strategy. It is a way to calm

children so they can sleep.

DE MONTE

Are you not a child?

Don Juan's eyes flare at this. There is fight in his eyes. But he keeps his composure.

DON JUAN

I do not need a wet nurse.

DE MONTE

No, Don Juan. What you need is good, Godly council.

DON JUAN

Everyone calls upon God. No one calls upon himself.

DE MONTE

It is not about us calling on ourselves. It is about God calling upon us to do his will.

DON JUAN

If we are the ones to do it, why call on him? Why not just get it done?

DE MONTE

Because unless the Lord builds the house, they labor in vain who build it. Unless the Lord guards the city, the watchman stays awake in vain. I know you are a man of action. And that is good. But now you must also be a man of faith. Pray, Don Juan. And I will pray for you.

He stands to leave. His mug of ale, still full, sits on the table.

DON JUAN (gesturing to the ale)

Aren't you forgetting something?

DE MONTE

I don't drink, but when doing business in a pub it is polite to purchase the product. You are welcome to drink it if you wish. Or to avoid it if you are able.

He turns and walks out.

Don Juan fumes. Picks up his ale. Looks at it. Puts it down. Leaves.

EXT. PUB - NIGHT

Don Juan steps out of the pub. He starts to walk away when someone calls out his name. He turns to see the announcer from the meeting at the Vatican.

ANNOUNCER

Don Juan! I thought I would find you here.

DON JUAN

Why did you think you would find me here?

ANNOUNCER

Well, in truth I was told to look here. And if you weren't here I was told to look at the popina or cabaret.

DON JUAN Who told you this?

The announcer hesitates. Fidgets. Don Juan is obviously offended.

ANNOUNCER

My apologies, señore.

DON JUAN

Who told you to seek me at pubs and taverns?

Another pause. Uncomfortable.

ANNOUNCER

His Holiness. He told me I would find you here. Or at a cabaret.

DON JUAN

The Pope? He told you to look for me here?

ANNOUNCER He wishes to see you in the morning. He wants to show you something.

DON JUAN

I must have some reputation for him to think -

ANNOUNCER Please, Don Juan. Do not be offended. His Holiness has requested your presence. First thing in the morning.

Another long pause.

Then.

DON JUAN

Very well. You have delivered your message. You may go.

ANNOUNCER

May I assist you in any way?

DON JUAN

Yes. Tell His Holiness I had only a half mug of ale, turned down an offer for a free mug of ale, and that I will not be at the bar this evening as I have an important engagement first thing tomorrow.

The announcer tries to hide an amused smile.

ANNOUNCER I will deliver your message, señore.

A slight bow, and he walks away.

Don Juan looks back at the pub. Sighs. Walks off in the opposite direction.

INT. GUEST SUITE - NIGHT

A suite fit for a king. Large, well appointed, with artwork adorning the walls and furniture one might find in a palace.

A window overlooks the Vatican.

Philip sits in bed, writing with a dip pen on a piece of parchment paper.

A loud banging at the door.

He sighs.

The banging continues.

He puts the pen and parchment away. Goes to the door.

He opens it to reveal Don Juan, looking tired.

Philip regards him a moment, then steps aside for him to enter.

INT. GUEST SUITE - NIGHT

Philip and Don Juan sit across from each other in large chairs.

> DON JUAN
>
> What do they think of me? Really.

> PHILIP
>
> You are young. You are brash. You may well lead us to our deaths.

> DON JUAN
>
> Then why was it so easy for them to approve me as admiral.

> PHILIP They fought

it.

DON JUAN

Not hard. I want to know why. If they don't trust me, why make me admiral?

PHILIP

Because you are young. Because you are brash. Because they think you can be manipulated.

Don Juan takes this in. Bristles.

DON JUAN

So they want me to be a puppet.

> PHILIP Yes.

> DON JUAN
>
> And you? Am I to be your puppet?

PHILIP

When have I ever made you feel that you were in any way inferior to me?

DON JUAN

So then you trust me? To make my own judgments?
PHILIP
With the right council, yes.

DON JUAN

With the right manipulators, you mean.

PHILIP Don Juan. Please. I have councilors. No one can lead a nation, or an armada, without wise council. We are not God. In the multitude of councilors there is wisdom.

DON JUAN In the multitude of councilors there is wisdom. I like that.

PHILIP

You should. It is from the Bible. One of the greatet councilors.

Don Juan takes a long breath.

DON JUAN
I know you want me to be a man of faith. I know you want me to be God's man for the job. But I don't think I can be.
PHILIP
I trust you, Don Juan. I do not know if you are God's choice. I pray that you are.

DON JUAN And if I am not?

PHILIP
Then he will deal with it. You have a duty to do. Do your best, with whatever you have. Trust God with the rest.

DON JUAN I hope I can.

PHILIP
You may not have another choice.

EXT. APOSTOLIC PALACE - DAY

The sun is just peeking over distant hills. The city is a dancing mix of reds and oranges and yellows as the rising sun moves across the buildings.

Don Juan stands outside, watching the morning unfold.

A procession of well armed carriages and chariots march by.

In the midst of the procession, a carriage pulls up next to him. The door opens. Inside is Pope Pius. He motions for Don Juan to join him.

POPE PIUS V

Good morning, Don Juan. Please. Come with me.

INT. CARRIAGE - DAY

Don Juan sits next to Pope Pius as the carriage rumbles along on its way.

DON JUAN

Where are we going?

POPE PIUS V

We will be gone for several days. Clothing and all other needs have been provided for you.

DON JUAN But ...

POPE PIUS V You will see, Don

Juan. All in God's timing.

EXT. VATICAN - DAY

The procession marches off, out of the Vatican, to the east.

EXT. COUNTRYSIDE - DAY

The procession is stopped.

Soldiers and other officials eat. Don Juan among them.

Don Juan looks around. Walks among the soldiers and officials.

At the edge of the procession he sees a group of soldiers gathered in what appears to be an official formation. They are not eating.

He approaches them. They form a line to prevent him from passing.

DON JUAN

I was just -

Behind them, looking between their shoulders, he sees Pope Pius kneeling in prayer.

DON JUAN (CONT'D) It's ok. I'll just

go back.

INT. CARRIAGE - DAY

Don Juan once again rides next to Pope Pius. They ride in silence for a while. Then:

DON JUAN How often do you

pray, Your Holiness?

POPE PIUS V

Not often enough. And yourself?

DON JUAN

Less often than that. Pope Pius smiles.

POPE PIUS V

With your current charge, you will either learn to pray or be driven to it.

EXT. LORETTO, ITALY - DAY

A small hillside town overlooking the ocean. Trees compete with scrub brush, each trying to lay claim to the territory.

Homes of brick and mortar spot the hills. Smoke rises from wood stoves.

Ahead, atop a hill, is what appears to be a walled city within the city.

The procession approaches the walls and snakes its way inside them.

INT. HOLY HOUSE OF LORETO - DAY

Pope Pius and Don Juan enter a small brick house that is set inside a larger cathedral.

Don Juan takes in the sight.

The house is simple and squat, sparse compared to the building that encases it.

Pope Pius crosses himself. Says a prayer. Turns to Don Juan.

> POPE PIUS V
>
> Welcome to this holy place, Don Juan.
>
> DON JUAN What is this?
>
> POPE PIUS V
>
> This is the holy house of Loreto.
>
> It was in this house that the
>
> Virgin Mary, mother of our Lord and Savior, was born and raised.

Don Juan looks about. Squints at the Pope.

DON JUAN

> With respect, Your Holiness. Even a man of the world like
> me knows that the Holy Mother was not born in Italy.
>
> POPE PIUS V This house was moved in
> a single night, by God's holy angels, from Palestine to
> this very spot, in order to protect it from the enemies
> of God.
>
> DON JUAN Is that

true?

Pope Pius smiles.

> POPE PIUS V
>
> It definitively was not moved, brick by
> brick, during the Crusades, by the Angeli family. The
> records are clear. Countless eyewitnesses observed three
> angels carrying the three-walled home of Sts. Joachim and
> Anne, the home of the Holy Family in Nazareth, because
> our Lord did not want His home profaned by the Saracen
> conquerors.

Don Juan returns his smile.

DON JUAN

Seeing is believing.

POPE PIUS V

Is it not better to believe we may be instruments of God's will as much as the holy angels?

DON JUAN

Perhaps. But do you believe that man can aspire to be of service to God?

POPE PIUS V

What I believe is not important. What is important is what you believe. Do you believe in God, Don Juan?

DON JUAN Of course, papa.

POPE PIUS V

Do you believe he has called you to this mission?

A long pause. Don Juan walks to the small altar. Feels along its edge with a few fingers.

DON JUAN

I am a man of the world, Your Holiness. I do not know that God would call me to dinner, let alone to be master of his fleet.

POPE PIUS V

David was an adulterer. And a murderer. Yet God called him to lead a nation.

DON JUAN

I want to believe. But how can I, when so many others do not? Only you, and my brother. And I am not sure if he really believes or if he only wants me there as his puppet.

POPE PIUS V

I believe, Don Juan. And what is more important, God believes.

Don Juan looks around the small house. He walks to a wall and places his hand on the stones. Pope Pius watches him for a moment.

POPE PIUS V (CONT'D) You still have questions.

DON JUAN

I still ... But which is it, Your Holiness? What is the truth of this place?

Pope Pius takes a moment to respond. The tone has changed. No more banter. It's time for earnest talk.

POPE PIUS V

When Acre fell, in 1291, it was clear that the Ottomans would stop at nothing to destroy every vestige of Christianity. This house, the home of our Blessed Mother, would have been at the top of their list.

DON JUAN

Hence it was moved, I understand.

But by whom?

POPE PIUS V

Acre had fallen, Don Juan. Our last outpost in the region was gone. God's armies were no longer able to save themselves, let alone move an entire building.

DON JUAN

So it was the angels?

POPE PIUS V

To preserve this place, God sent his angels to carry it here. His angels brought this holy house here in a single night, before his enemies could destroy it. Any other means would have failed. Defenders would have been killed and the house destroyed. Moving it brick by brick would have taken too long and the enemy would have been upon them. Only God could have moved this place, and he sent his angels to do it.

DON JUAN

Then why refer to that story about the Angeli family?

POPE PIUS V

That story was started by men who cannot believe in miracles. There are many today who do not. But God still performs miracles, and he still sends his angels to help us.

DON JUAN

Then why not just send his angels to defeat the Turks now?

POPE PIUS V

Perhaps he will. And perhaps you will be there to witness it.

He walks to the altar and kneels.

POPE PIUS V (CONT'D) Pray with me.

Don Juan crosses to the altar and kneels next to him.

The Pope's lips move in silent prayer.

Don Juan stares at the ground. His lips do not move.

EXT. HOLY HOUSE OF LORETO - DAY

Don Juan and the Pope sit together, eating a modest meal. Soldiers surround them.

All throughout the area, the Pope's entourage eats. Soldiers keep one eye on their food and one wary eye on their surroundings.

DON JUAN

We should go soon. I have a fleet to build.

POPE PIUS V

You are always at the ready, Don Juan. This is good. But sometimes we are ready before God is.

DON JUAN

When will he be ready?

POPE PIUS V

He will let you know. Just take care not to charge ahead before him.

EXT. SHIP YARD, GENOA ITALY - DAY

A city nestled in the hills above a stark blue sea. Tucked inside a deep bay, workers labor building wooden ships.

The sun glints off steel weaponry as it is transported onto ships that are already built.

Shouts are heard from the laborers. Periodic gunfire is heard in the distance.

Philip stands watching workers bring together the ribs of a new galleyass. Next to him is GIOVANNI ANDREA DORIA, long face, sharp nose, eyes that have seen defeat.

PHILIP

I expect he will be brash at times. He lacks much, but he has a lion's heart.

DORIA

I will guide him well, Philip.

PHILIP

And may God guide you both.

A procession of chariots and carriages, well armed and with the papal banner flying, approaches them from the city.

They watch the procession approach, and stand tall as it stops in front of them.

The door of a carriage opens. Don Juan starts to get out, but Pope Pius puts a hand on his shoulder.

Don Juan stops and turns to him.

Philip and Doria watch as the Pope places his hand on Don Juan's head and gives him a blessing they do not hear.

After this, Don Juan exits, the carriage door closes, and the procession snakes away.

Don Juan stands looking out at the shipyard, then approaches Philip and Doria.

PHILIP (CONT'D)

Don Juan. May I present your second in command, Giovanni
Andrea Doria, Knight Commander of the Order of Santiago.

Doria gives Don Juan a slight bow.

DORIA

Your servant, sir.

DON JUAN

I'm glad of your assistance, Knight Commander.

He turns and surveys the ships being built, the ships already assembled, and the weaponry and armor being loaded aboard.

DON JUAN (CONT'D) Is this our
fleet, then?

DORIA

A portion of it, sir. We are to sail with two hundred six
galleys and six galleyasses.

DON JUAN And to
man them?

PHILIP

Rowers and artillery are being recruited.

We could not supply them from the League?

DORIA

Some of the compliment are current soldiers, yes. But our needs
for a fleet this size requires recruiting from other sources.

DON JUAN Conscription?

PHILIP

Some, yes. But we are hopeful that a fair wage will be
attractive to men who need work.

More gunfire rattles in the distance.

DON JUAN

And what battle is that I hear?

Doria smiles.

DORIA

Come and see. I think you will be pleased.

EXT. HILLTOP - DAY

Don Juan and Doria ride on horses over the crest of a green hill. They stop at the peak and look down.

Just below them is a line of artillerymen, each with two muzzle loading rifles.

Behind each artilleryman is another man. These men seem less regal in their bearing. Less kempt somehow.

A man in Venetian military uniform rides back and forth in front of them on a tall horse. He shouts orders that are heard but unintelligible from where Don Juan and Doria sit atop the hill.

The artillerymen turn, in formation, and raise one rifle each. Then men behind them hold their second rifles at the ready.

At a command from their leader, the artillerymen fire a round from their rifles, then hand the rifle back to the man behind them.

The rifles are exchanged. As the artillerymen take aim and fire again, the men behind them rapidly load the second rifle.

The artillerymen make the swap again, and the process repeats.

After several rounds, the process slows, the loaders unable to keep up with the rate of fire. Some are better than others, and the gunfire goes from uniform to scattered.

The leader shouts again, and the firing stops.

DORIA

When the ships enter battle, and the rifles are fired, this new process will enable us to continue firing without hesitation.

DON JUAN

We may need three rifles and two loaders.

DORIA

What we have will suffice. The truth is that when they are aboard ships, tossed in the waves and under fire themselves, it will take them longer to aim and fire. That will give the loaders more time to load and they should be able to keep up.

DON JUAN

But with the ships tossed in the waves, it will take the loaders longer to load.

Doria takes a long look at Don Juan. Then looks down at the scene below, where the firing has started again.

DORIA

That is an excellent observation, Don Juan. I can see why God has chosen you to lead us.

DON JUAN

The leaders of the Holy League chose me.

DORIA

Trust in God, Don Juan. He works in mysterious ways.

And the Holy League is perhaps the most mysterious of all.

Doria and Don Juan share a good laugh at this.

DORIA

One of life's grand mysteries. How will you keep this group

from fighting themselves?

DON JUAN

From what I know of them, it would take a miracle.

DORIA

I think you are right.

DON JUAN

Then let us pray that God is on our side.

DORIA

Better yet, let us pray that we are on his;.

Doria turns his horse and rides back over the hill. Don Juan watches the scene below for a moment.

He looks back in the direction Doria went.

Looks to the sky.

Looks down. Mouths something we cannot hear. Crosses himself. Turns and rides away.

INT. PRISON - DAY

Inside stark walls a group of ROUGH MEN are gathered, surrounded by guards with military bearing.

Don Juan walks before them.

Some of the men stand, some sit on the hard ground. None of them look interested.

DON JUAN

Any of you willing to fight for the cause of God may take leave of

this place today.

PRISONER 1

If we were on the side of God, we wouldn't be here!

The other prisoners laugh. Don Juan smiles.

DON JUAN Perhaps I should look in a

monastery. Perhaps those men would be braver than

this lot.

The prisoners murmur at the insult. A few of the ones sitting on the ground stand, and look like they might charge.

The guards quickly move to intercept.

PRISONER 2

Careful who you call cowards, Don Juan. Should we care to defend our courage, even these guards could not protect you.

DON JUAN

So you will fight for your honor, but not for God?

PRISONER 3

We will fight for our freedom!

The other prisoners cheer at this.

DON JUAN

If you join us, you will be freed this day.

PRISONER 1

Freed to what? The chains of an oar? Freed to fight a battle that is not ours? What kind of freedom is that?

DON JUAN

Fight for your honor then. If you survive you will be free to return home, and you be honored among men and God.

PRISONER 1

We don't need to seek honor. Here we have honor among thieves.

The prisoners laugh and cheer.

Don Juan smiles again.

I am sorry to have troubled you. Go back to the honor of your cells. God will provide soldiers for the battle.

He turns to go. Three guards escort him. One of the prisoners stands and walks after him.

PRISONER 4

I will go, Don Juan. I will fight with you.

Don Juan stops and looks at the man.

DON JUAN What is your name?

PRISONER 4

Enrico, sir. Enrico de Solando.

DON JUAN

Welcome to God's army, Enrico.

Enrico smiles and bows.

ENRICO

It is my honor, sir.

Don Juan, Enrico, and the guards walk out.

EXT. GENOA ITALY - DAY

Doria rides a horse in front of a line of people. They all wear worn clothes and listen intently.

DORIA

I cannot guarantee your safety. I can only guarantee that
you will be paid and you will be well fed. And that, come what
may, God himself will regard you with honor.

A woman steps forward from the back.

WOMAN

And what of us women? How will we fend while our hus-
bands are away fighting your fight?

My lady, this is God's fight. All who sacrifice lives or loved
ones will be cared for by the Lord Himself.

The woman huffs. Whatever.

A man steps from the crowd.

MAN

And if we go? If we fight? What will be our wages?

DORIA

Your wages will be fair, but your honor great.

MAN

Honor does not feed my family, Señor Doria.

DORIA

God will provide.

MAN

God barely provides now. How will he provide if I am
not here?

DORIA

Perhaps God barely provides because you barely trust
him. If God calls you, trust him and fight with us. If he does
not, stay and fight for your family. But if he calls, and you do
not answer, I cannot say what will be your end.

Doria turns his horse to go.

DORIA (CONT'D) Any man who wishes to
honor God and defend his kingdom may come to the harbor
and join us. Pray that you do his will.

He rides away.

The crowd murmurs. Disperses.

A few men walk in the direction Doria rode away.

INT. CAPTAIN'S DINING ROOM - NIGHT

A dining room aboard a large fragata. A simple meal sits, partially eaten, on the table before Don Juan and Doria.

Half empty glasses of wine sit on the table next to the food.

Don Juan chews slowly, looking down at the table.

Doria looks at him. Gestures to get his attention.

> DORIA
>
> Something on your mind, Don Juan?

> DON JUAN
>
> Recruitment is too slow.

> DORIA It will

come.

> DON JUAN
>
> We don't have enough men to man the ships we have, let
alone those being built.

> DORIA
>
> The recruits will come, Don Juan. They are being recruited
in all the nations of the League. They will be here.

> DON JUAN
>
> I pray you are right.

> DORIA
>
> And the Venetian ships will be fully manned. The Doge
of Venice himself has guaranteed it.

Don Juan scoffs.

> DON JUAN
>
> Then we can be sure they will be half manned and un-
prepared.

> DORIA
>
> Then we will provide recruits and training.

> DON JUAN
>
> There is no time. We have a duty to Famagusta.
> Our duty is to God.

> DON JUAN And he has, through the
Pope, informed us that his will is that we rescue Famagusta.

DORIA

Famagusta will be fine. They are heavily reinforced from land. Besides, militarily and geographically, they are near impossible to defeat.

DON JUAN My history lessons tell me we thought the same about Acre.

DORIA

Almost three hundred years have passed since then. We know more. We have more skills. Better weaponry. Better strategy.

DON JUAN As do the Turks.

DORIA   God is with us.

DON JUAN

The same God who was with Acre when it fell?

DORIA

Do you not trust God, Don Juan?
Don Juan chews another bite, slowly. Takes his time answering.

DON JUAN

I do not trust the Venetians.
Doria has a good laugh at this.

DORIA

Then the wisdom of God is upon you!
Don Juan smiles.

DON JUAN

It doesn't take the wisdom of the Almighty to know that.
They share a moment here. Doria sips his wine. Sits back and regards Don Juan.
DORIA

You didn't answer my question?

DON JUAN What?

DORIA

Do you trust God?

Another pause while Don Juan considers.

DON JUAN

I don't know. I want to trust him. But I don't know if I can.

DORIA

What holds you back?

DON JUAN

Look at me. Would you trust a God who put me in charge?

DORIA

He didn't put you in charge, Don Juan. He is still in charge.

You are his servant.

Another pause. Don Juan finishes his wine.

DON JUAN

Then let us pray I serve him well.

EXT. SHIP, COAST OF CORFU - DAY

Don Juan stands at the bow of a large galley, surveying the ships and the sea beyond. Doria stands next to him.

Oarsmen and other soldiers mill about on the ships. Some polish artillery. Some talk amongst themselves. Some play cards on the decks of the ships.

Ashore, the business of daily life continues.

DON JUAN

I told you I don't trust Venetians.

The Doge will be here, Don Juan. Have faith.

DON JUAN

It is not faith I lack. It is ships and men to sail them.

DORIA

Gideon lacked an entire army, yet God gave him victory.

DON JUAN

Then perhaps we should sail without Venier.

DORIA

> I think in this case it would be unwise. The Holy League is a tenuous arrangement. Political affronts could divide loyalties and undermine our cause.

DON JUAN

> I wouldn't mind being divided from Venier.

DORIA

> A house divided cannot stand. We unite ourselves to each other under God, and trust in his loyalty rather than our own.

DON JUAN

> It is hard to trust a God who pairs you with a Venetian.

They share a good laugh at this.

DORIA

Faith is sometimes difficult.

DON JUAN

> Meanwhile I think it best not to sit idle. We need to move this fleet away from Corfu, lest the conscripted men find better options ashore.

DORIA

> I'll have a letter dispatched to Venier post haste. And where should he meet us?

We'll set sail for the bay of
Gomenizza at first wind tomorrow.

DORIA

Gomenizza. Very good choice. The men won't find any better options there.

DON JUAN Please ensure we are fully provisioned. I do not want any more delays than Venier has already caused us.

EXT. BAY OF GOMENIZZA - DAY

Don Juan's fleet sails into the bay, the Papal flag high. Beneath the Papal flag on each ship is the flag of the ship's origin, and beneath that the flags of the crew members.

This results in some ships with four or more flags.

INT. CAPTAIN'S QUARTERS - DAY

Don Juan sits at his chart table, composing a letter with a dip pen and parchment paper. A knock at the door.

DON JUAN Come.

The door opens to reveal Enrico, the lone recruit from the prison Don Juan visited personally.

DON JUAN (CONT'D) Enrico. How

good to see you. How can I help you?

ENRICO

Señor, the Venetian ships have arrived.

Don Juan scowls. Stands. Looks out the porthole of his cabin. Squints into the sun.

DON JUAN Finally.

ENRICO

It may not be all you hoped for, señor.

Don Juan turns back to Enrico.

DON JUAN How bad

is it?

ENRICO

It is better if you see.

Enrico turns and leaves.

Don Juan follows him out.

EXT. SMALL BOAT - DAY

Don Juan rides in a small boat, inspecting the Venetian vessels.

They are war torn and in need of much repair. Sails are ripped. Masts are broken. Some of the ships list in the sea.

Their crews look ragged and hungry.

Don Juan fumes.

INT. CAPTAIN'S DINING ROOM - DAY

Don Juan and Venier stand at Don Juan's dining table. Don Juan fumes. Venier boils.

DON JUAN

This is what you bring me after all these months?

VENIER

While you have been playing at war, my crew has been in battle.

DON JUAN

The battle is for Famagusta. This was the agreement.

VENIER

The battle is where it finds us, Admiral.

He says 'Admiral' like he means something else.

And your crew? I see barely enough men to handle half
your ships, and those I see look to be wasting away.

VENIER

A few weeks and our men will be refreshed. Our ships will
be repaired.

DON JUAN

I have had too many delays already! Famagusta awaits our
reinforcements!
The door opens and Doria steps in.

DORIA

Famagusta no longer requires our assistance, Don Juan.
DON JUAN Do not
tell me.
DORIA I must.
A long pause.
DON JUAN Speak then.

DORIA

Famagusta is lost. It's ground laid waste, it's walls burned, it's men
tortured and killed, its women and children taken as slaves.

DON JUAN

(to Venier)
This is your doing. Your delays have cost us our last pos-
session in Cyprus, and God alone knows how many souls.

VENIER

You could have sailed without me, if God was with you.
Don Juan gives Doria the side eye.

DON JUAN

> I was advised to wait.

VENIER

> It is just as well. You could not have saved Famagusta.

DON JUAN

> You cannot know what we would have done there.

VENIER

> If God wanted Famagusta saved, then he would have saved it.

DON JUAN

> We are the instruments of his will. If we fail, so does his desire for us.

Venier laughs. It's not a nice laugh.

VENIER

> Get down from the altar, Admiral. You are no servant of God.

DON JUAN

> It was he who chose me to lead.

VENIER

> I trust no God who would choose the likes of you to lead a fleet.

Don Juan fumes. Starts to lunge. Doria stops him.

DORIA

> Not now, Don Juan. The men cannot perceive dissension among the leadership.

Don Juan fumes a moment more, then backs up.

DORIA (CONT'D)

> (to Venier)
> I think it is best you leave now.

Venier smiles and gives a slight bow to Doria. He does not acknowledge Don Juan.

VENIER

> (to Doria)
> Keep your dog on a leash, commander, or we may all get bitten.

He walks out.

> That man will be the death of us all.

DORIA

> If God wills, he may indeed.

EXT. DON JUAN'S FRAGATA - DAY

Don Juan stands amidships on his fragata.

The ship is rowed among the fleet. Officers and soldiers alike stand at the gunwales of their ships as he addresses them.

Venier stands with his men, sneering.

Don Juan addresses the ships as he passes.

> DON JUAN It is here that we test our pre-
> paredness. Soon we will test our mettle. I expect all men to
> fight with honor, in service of the Most High God. Today
> you are playing a game. Soon you will be at war. Pray that
> you are prepared.

EXT. DON JUAN'S FARGATA - DAY

Don Juan and Doria once again stand at the bow, watching over the fleet.

The various ships row and sail out, assuming battle formations.

> DON JUAN
>
> I am hopeful, but unsure.
>
> DORIA
>
> It is their first time serving together with live fire. It will
> take some time, but they will establish a rhythm.
>
> DON JUAN And if they
>
> don't?
>
> DORIA
>
> They will do it here or in war. The pressures of live battle tend
> to create a camaraderie.
>
> (MORE)

DORIA (CONT'D)

> For one to survive he must depend on the others, and the
> others must depend on him.
>
> DON JUAN
>
> Then let's see what we have to work with.

He turns and signals to a cannon crew behind him. The crew angels the cannon up, and fires.

Out at sea, live fire begins exploding from the ships.

Some ships fire out to sea. Some pull back and fire towards land.

A shot strikes the bow of Don Juan's ship, causing him and Doria to leap back and fall to the deck.

Don Juan leaps up and shouts.

> DON JUAN (CONT'D) Pull back! Pull
>
> back!

INT. DON JUAN'S FRAGATA - DAY

Below deck, the oarsmen row hard, pulling the ship away from the war games.

EXT. DON JUAN'S FRAGATA - DAY

Don Juan and Doria stand at the bow, watching the war games recede as their ship pulls back to a safer distance.

DORIA

At least we know they can hit something.

DON JUAN

Let's hope they are at least as effective against the enemy.

INT. CAPTAIN'S QUARTERS - DAY

Don Juan sits at his chart table, mapping out a course. Outside, the sounds of live fire continue.

The door to his quarters burst open and Doria rushes in.

DORIA

Don Juan! Come quickly!

EXT. DON JUAN'S FRAGATA - DAY

Don Juan and Doria rush up to the deck and look out towards the live fire exercises.

One of the ships has disengaged from the exercise. It drifts out, a brawl raging on its deck.

The other ships edge away from the drifting vessel, and all firing of artillery stops.

Don Juan turns to the crew of his own ship, who stand watching the incident.

DON JUAN Get us

there! Now!

EXT. SHIP - DAY

Don Juan's ship pulls up alongside the drifting vessel. He and Doria leap across and board it.

The fighting has stopped. Men are injured, and stand facing each other as if the battle may flare up at any moment.

DON JUAN

What is this? Do we fight for God or do we fight against

ourselves?

Behind him, Venier appears, running towards him.

Don Juan whirls on him. Fumes.

DON JUAN (CONT'D) I might

have known you would instigate dissension.

Venire holds up his hands. Bows to Don Juan.

VENIER

This was not my doing, Admiral.

DON JUAN

This is your vessel. You are responsible.

VENIER

And I will take responsibility.

DON JUAN Then do so!

VENIER

Admiral. Your patience. There is a longstanding quarrel between Venetians and Hapsburgs, and it is you who put them
together on this ship.

DON JUAN

Because there were not enough
Venetians left after your failures.

VENIER

After the fury of war! Our men fought your enemies while
you sat back and prepared! While you were planning, we were
fighting!

DON JUAN

And now you bring that fight to a mutiny! Enough! This is
treason and these men will be hanged!

VENIER

For the sake of Christ take no such action unless you want
me to sink your galley and all on board! I will bring these
dogs to heel!

Don Juan turns to Doria. Doria motions for him to follow. They step away a few feet.

DORIA

This is his ship, Admiral. And his crew.

DON JUAN And my

fleet.

DORIA

Be that as it may. Let him manage this. Give him the
authority over his own vessels and men.

Don Juan turns and looks back at Venier.

A tense moment.

Don Juan steps forward.

DON JUAN

(to Venier)

See that you deal with these men according to their sins. You
have twenty four hours to do so.

(MORE)

DON JUAN (CONT'D)

And if you cannot, then I will take command. If these men will
not fear God, let them fear Don Juan.

EXT. DON JUAN'S FRAGATA - DAY

The sun sets over the sea.

The ships sit at repose in the bay.

Don Juan stands at the bow, drinking a glass of wine. Doria stands with him.

Some distance away Venier's vessel sits at anchor. Three men hang from the yardarms.

DON JUAN

We've yet to see a single enemy and already we've lost men to battle.

DORIA

We have seen an enemy.

DON JUAN Venier.

DORIA

No. Not Venier. The devil himself. He will cause division
and violence anywhere he can to stop us.

DON JUAN

Then perhaps this is a good thing.

DORIA How so?

DON JUAN

If the devil would work so hard to defeat us here, perhaps he
knows we are destined for victory.

EXT. VENIER'S SHIP - NIGHT

Venier stands at the stern, looking out over the sea. He glares directly at Don Juan's fragata.

VENIER

You will fail, Don Juan, but I will not be sunk with you.

INT. CAPTAIN'S DINING ROOM - NIGHT

Don Juan and Doria sit at dinner. Don Juan picks at his food. Doria regards him as he chews.

DORIA

What has spoiled your appetite, Don Juan?

Don Juan takes a long breath. Fidgets his food around the plate. Takes a sip of wine.

DON JUAN

I wonder. That is all. I wonder.

DORIA

We all wonder. But usually we wonder about something
specific.

Don Juan stands and crosses to a portal. Look out. Turns back to Doria.

DON JUAN

Do you believe my commission is from God?

DORIA

What I believe does not matter. Only what you believe
matters.

DON JUAN

I have heard that before. But I wonder. If it is not God's will, it
doesn't matter if I believe it is.

DORIA

And if it is his will, it wouldn't matter if you didn't.

DON JUAN

Not true. Not true at all.

DORIA Tell me.

DON JUAN

If it is God's will that I lead this mission, and that we succeed, all I must do is obey. I need not believe. Only obey.

DORIA

Obedience is its own form of faith, yes.

DON JUAN But if it is not his will, and I believe it is, then I will charge ahead without his grace. I will lead us all to our deaths.

DORIA

The Pope himself believes you are God's choice. Why do you hesitate?

DON JUAN

Many things. Usually small things. But now ... Those three men hanging from the yardarm of Venier's vessel. We have yet to engage our enemy and already we are losing men.

DORIA But you have gained Venier.

DON JUAN Have I?

DORIA If Venier were not with you, he would not have hanged those traitors. He would have congratulated them on fighting the Hapsburgs and sailed away to join the Ottomans.

DON JUAN I still don't trust him.

DORIA Then trust God.

DON JUAN Also not easy.

DORIA

It never was. It may never be. But God does not call us to trust him on the easy path. He calls us to trust him to make a way where there is no way.

DON JUAN Paths in the wilderness. Rivers in the desert.

DORIA

You know your scriptures.

DON JUAN

Part of my upbringing.

DORIA

Then let that upbringing serve you well. Recall God's faithfulness to his people, and perhaps you will believe in his faithfulness to you.

DON JUAN To us.

DORIA To all of

us.

DON JUAN

It will take time, but it appears I will have the time I need.
We need to sail back to Corfu and winter there. The campaign
season is over. We will strike out again in the spring.

EXT. DON JUAN'S FRAGATA - DAY

Don Juan watches over the redistribution of supplies and ammunition among the ships.
Men move food, artillery, and assorted goods on and off ships all around the bay.
Venier approaches from behind.

VENIER Don Juan!

Don Juan turns to see Venier pointing out over the edge of a high point on the bay. In the distance he can just make out three masts moving along the horizon.

EXT. SHIP - DAY

Don Juan and Venier watch the masts through a telescope.

DON JUAN

How far away would you guess?

VENIER

A mile. Not more than two.

DON JUAN

Find Doria. Get the ships ready.

EXT. SHIP - DAY

Don Juan stands at the bow, artillery cannons at the ready. Below deck, oarsmen move the ship into position.

The other ships of the fleet have taken up positions in a naval formation, lines and flanks ready to do battle.

Don Juan watches through the telescope as the first of the ships rounds into the bay.

Flying high is a Cretan flag.

From the next ship over, Doria calls out to him.

DORIA

They are from Crete!

DON JUAN

The ships are from Crete! But who is in command?

Doria raises his telescope.

Don Juan does the same.

TELESCOPE VIEW: A crew of men work the deck, while sails fly and oars give them aid.

Standing at the bow is NICOLO ENRIZO, battle hardened captain, telescope held to his face.

He waves.

END TELESCOPE VIEW

DON JUAN (CONT'D) It's Enrizo!

EXT. SHIP - DAY

Two of the fleet's ships, one under Don Juan and one under Doria, come alongside Enrizo's vessel.

The vessel is war torn and weather beaten.

Enrizo calls out to Don Juan.

ENRIZO

I had a mind to find safe harbor and repair what is left of

our fleet, but I have urgent news for you!

INT. CAPTAIN'S QUARTERS - DAY

Enrizo, Don Juan, Venier, and Doria sit in the captain's quarters. It's cramped with all four in there.

DORIA

You are positive?

ENRIZO

Yes. The entire Ottoman fleet has left. They intend to

winter at Lepanto and repair their ships there.

DON JUAN

How much repair do they need?

ENRIZO

They won the battle, but took heavy losses. There is a good

deal of damage, and they need to replenish their soldiers.

Don Juan ponders this for a moment.

DON JUAN

Could we catch them before they reach Lepanto?

ENRIZO

No. They left three days before we did. They are likely in

Lepanto already.

DON JUAN

With a diminished fleet.

DORIA

Don Juan, you cannot be considering this.

DON JUAN

God has opened an opportunity.

VENIER

For what? For our death?

DON JUAN The Ottoman fleet is

heavily damaged. They are short on men.

DORIA

By the time we get there they will have repaired their fleet and recruited more men.

VENIER

If we get there at all. The season has changed. Even the Ottomans won't campaign in winter.

DORIA

He is right. The winds would be against us. The seas would be averse.

DON JUAN

When the disciple's boat was rocked in the storm, Jesus calmed the seas.

VENIER

You claim to be Jesus now?

DON JUAN

No. But if he has called us to victory, he will calm the seas for us.

VENIER

The Ottomans will be in the same seas, Don Juan. You cannot calm the seas for one and not for all.

A long pause. A tense moment waiting for Don Juan. Then:

DON JUAN

I do not ask you to follow me. I ask you to follow God. Let us all retire and wrestle in prayer till morning. Then we will make our decision.

Doria and Venier glance at each other.

VENIER

If God be in it, let him show us as we pray.

He and Doria walk out. Enrizo stays behind.

ENRIZO

They are right, Don Juan. It is a dangerous thing to take up a naval campaign this late in the year.

(MORE)

ENRIZO (CONT'D)

You risk losing your fleet before you fire a shot.

DON JUAN

It was a dangerous thing for a boy to fight a giant. Pray, Enrizo. Pray.

EXT. DON JUAN'S FRAGATA - DAY

Don Juan stands starboard, looking out over the fleet. A breeze blows through his hair. The seas are calm.

Venier steps up next to him.

> VENIER
>
> I have one question.

> DON JUAN
>
> Then ask what you came to ask.

> VENIER
>
> Is this for God's glory, or for yours.

> DON JUAN
>
> I have the same question. I pray that it is for his.

> VENIER
>
> It seems to me that God would be more practical than to send a fleet to sea this late in the year.

> DON JUAN
>
> It seems to me he would be more practical than to send Gideon to face an army of thousands with only three hundred men.

> VENIER
>
> Gideon's men did not have to fight. Or to die. I don't expect we will be so blessed.

Don Juan takes this in. Turns to Venier.

> DON JUAN
>
> I cannot know the mind of God. I only know what I feel in my heart.

> VENIER
>
> And what is that?

> DON JUAN
>
> That this is the time to strike. This is God's open door. If we do not step through now, it may not open again.

Venier takes him in a moment. Nods.

> VENIER
>
> Then let us sail.

EXT. VATICAN - DAY

Pope Pius V walks among the Vatican gardens, admiring the plants and flowers in quiet contemplation.

A gentle breeze sways through the garden. The sun is bright. It is a pleasant day.

Pope Pius smiles as he takes it all in.

Behind him, Cardinal Carafa approaches, worry in his eyes.

> CARAFA Your Holi-
>
> ness.

Pope Pius turns to greet him. Smiles.

> POPE PIUS V

Good afternoon, Cardinal. Something troubles you?

> CARAFA

We have received word from Don Juan. They are sailing
to Lepanto to meet the Turks.

> POPE PIUS V

Good. Then pray that we soon hear of his victory.

> CARAFA

But Your Holiness ... To sail at this time, it is not done. The
season is too late.

> POPE PIUS V

It is the season for prayer, Cardinal. If God is for us, even
the seas cannot be against us.

EXT. VATICAN - DAY

Pope Pius stands in the window of his apartment, addressing a crowd.

> POPE PIUS V

On this day God has granted that our fleet will seek the
enemy in his own land. I call all Christians to prayer for
God's grace, protection, and blessing of our men as they seek
to do his will.

MONTAGE:

Cardinals pray throughout the Vatican.

Letters are received at churches throughout Europe.

Church bells ring.

Priests call parishioners to prayer.

Churches are filled with praying people.

People pray in their homes by candlelight.

END MONTAGE

EXT. OCEAN - DAY

MONTAGE OF SHOTS:

Top down shot of the large Holy League fleet sailing over a deep blue sea.

Views of bows cutting through the water.

Sails are full.

Oars push forward.

Flags wave atop masts.

EXT. GULF OF PATRAS - DAY

The Holy League fleet reaches the entrance of the Gulf of Patras. A large gulf, flanked on both
sides by mountainous terrain.

Islands line the entrance to the north, blocking the view of land behind them.

The Holy League ships pull up short and heave to at the entrance to the gulf.

To the west, the sun sets.

EXT. DON JUAN'S FRAGATA - NIGHT

Don Juan stands amidships, mouthing words we do not hear.

He crosses himself.

INT. CAPTAIN'S DINING ROOM - NIGHT

Don Juan eats alone. He chews slowly. He sips wine.

He stands and walks to the port hole.

> DON JUAN

I am doing all I can, Lord. I must trust you with the rest.

EXT. DON JUAN'S FRAGATA - DAY

Don Juan and Doria stand at the bow. A heavy fog lays over the gulf, obscuring the view.

> DORIA

They're here, Don Juan.

> DON JUAN

How can you be sure?

> DORIA

They would have retreated here after Famagusta for repairs and recruitment.

> DON JUAN

In this fog they could be on top of us.

> DORIA

They won't be. The fog is a detriment to us both. They won't fight until conditions are right.

Don Juan calls out to a sailor, PAULO, coiling rope nearby.

> DON JUAN Paulo!

Paulo drops his work and steps up to Don Juan.

> PAULO

At your service, Admiral.

> DON JUAN

You know Enrico, yes?

> PAULO   Of

course.

> DON JUAN

Find him. The two of you take one of the dinghies and set for those islands.

Paulo squints to see the islands through the fog.

> DON JUAN (CONT'D) Climb to the highest point and see what you can see.

> PAULO Yes, Admiral.

Paulo heads off below deck.

> DORIA

Sending spies to the Holy Land?

> DON JUAN

Let's hope they don't find giants.

EXT. VENIER'S FRAGATA - DAY

Venier stands at bow, watching through a telescope.

Through the fog, two masts can be seen approaching in the fog.

He puts down the telescope. Raises it. Looks again.

INT. CAPTAIN'S QUARTERS - DAY

Don Juan kneels in prayer.

A bang at the door.

Doria enters.

> DORIA

You need to come.

EXT. DON JUAN'S FRAGATA - DAY

Don Juan, Doria, and Venier stand at the bow. Don Juan holds the telescope to his eye.

> DON JUAN Only two?

> VENIER

Where there are two there are two hundred.

> DON JUAN

They've come to spy us out.

> DORIA

No. In this fog they can see us no better than we see them.

> DON JUAN Wait.

He stands watching a moment. Hands the telescope to Venier.

> VENIER

They're turning back.

> DORIA

I suspect they'll return to safe harbor behind the islands, turning their broadside to us as they reach it.

> DON JUAN

Then we can take them easily. We should go now.

> DORIA

It's a trap, Don Juan.

> DON JUAN

How can you be sure?

> DORIA

Because I know the Ottomans.

> DON JUAN I know

my God.

> VENIER

And they know theirs.

DORIA

Their ships have shallower drafts than ours. They can navigate the near shore where we would run aground on sand bars.

VENIER

They'd make simple work of us then.

DON JUAN

We can't simply wait. They have the advantage of land for provisions. They can wait us out while we starve.

VENIER

They won't. They're Ottomans. I guarantee you, Don Juan, as soon as the fog lifts, they'll be upon us.

Don Juan takes one more look through the telescope.

DON JUAN

Order the ships in formation. When they come, we'll be ready.

EXT. HILLTOP - DAY

Enrico and Paulo scurry their way up a hill on an island near the shore.

Below them, on the sea side of the island, their small rowboat sits nestled on the sandy beach.

Enrico crests the hill, staying low and keeping himself hidden as much as possible behind rocks and scrub.

Paulo crests a second later and follows.

Enrico peers through the branches of a scrub brush. His eyes go wide. He crosses himself.

Paulo sees Enrico's reaction and comes up to see what he sees.

ENRICO AND PAULO'S POV: A fleet of Ottoman ships stretch as far as the eye can see and beyond.

END POV

PAULO

How many do you think?

ENRICO

The admiral did not ask us to think.

He scurries down the far side of the hill, towards the ships. Paulo watches him for a moment. Looks back in the direction in which they came. Looks down the see Enrico descending towards enemy shores. Crosses himself. Follows Enrico.

EXT. GULF OF PATRAS - DAY

The ships move out into formation. As they separate the fog makes it difficult to see each other. They move in silence, even the sound of the oars in the water is muffled by the fog.

EXT. VENIER'S FRAGATA - DAY

Venier stands amidships, watching with a telescope.

Behind him, a uniformed Venetian officer, CARLO DeMARCO, steps up and looks out at the other ships fading into the fog.

DEMARCO

Do you think God will be with us?

VENIER

If he is with Don Juan, he is with us. If he is not, we are
on the left flank and can retreat quickly.

DEMARCO

Would we retreat so easily?

VENIER

If God is not in the battle, what choice do we have?

EXT. ISLAND SHORE - DAY

Enrico and Paulo crouch along the shore, hiding as best they can behind rocks and scrub brush.

They peer out at a massive navy.

On the ships, men work on sails, artillerymen practice their aim, and archers have their bows
at the ready.

How many do you count?

ENRICO

Two hundred fifty four so far. But we need to get further
along to see how many more there are.

EXT. ISLAND SHORE - DAY

Enrico and Paulo are further up the hill. The shore here is mostly beach, so they've had to climb
to find cover.

Paulo's foot slips, causing a large rock to tumble down. It carries smaller rocks with it.

Paulo slips several feet down the hillside.

EXT. OTTOMAN SHIP - DAY

Two Ottoman archers look up to see what the noise is from the island.

They see the rock and debris falling, and get their bows ready.

EXT. ISLAND SHORE - DAY

Enrico reaches down to take Paulo's hand.

ENRICO Are you al-

right?

PAULO Yes.

Enrico helps him back up the hill. For a moment, they slip out from behind the cover of the
rocks and scrub brush.

A shout from one of the ships startles them. They turn just in time to see arrows fly.

ENRICO Down!

They leap behind a rock as arrows tumble from the sky. One arrow falls directly behind the
rock that's hiding them, burying its tip in the ground less than a foot from Enrico.

We cannot stay here. They will come after us.

ENRICO

I hope Don Juan is praying for us.

They charge out from behind the rock and scurry up the hill, staying hidden as best they can.

EXT. SMALL BOAT - DAY

Enrico and Paulo shove their boat into the water. They jump in and start rowing towards the fleet.

They look up to see three red clad soldiers standing atop the hill, watching them.

INT. CAPTAIN'S QUARTERS - DAY

Don Juan sits at his table, studying charts, maps, and battle formations.

A loud knock at the door.

DON JUAN Come.

The door opens on Enrico and Paulo, both looking frazzled.

DON JUAN (CONT'D) I was beginning
to think you had defected to the enemy.

ENRICO
I am sorry for the delay, admiral. We walked the far shore
to count the ships in their fleet.

This gets Don Juan's attention.

DON JUAN How many
did you count?

Enrizo and Paulo look at each other.

DON JUAN (CONT'D) Just say it,
Enrico.

ENRICO
We counted two hundred fifty four.
But there were many more further in the bay. We could not
get close enough to those without being seen.

ENRICO We were
seen.

This gets Don Juan's attention.

DON JUAN And?

ENRICO
By the grace of God we escaped their arrows.

Don Juan nods. Stands. Shakes their hands.

DON JUAN
You have done well. May God's grace be upon you for your
courage.

PAULO
We are outnumbered, admiral.

ENRICO
By a significant number.

DON JUAN
Do not worry. If I have only one ship, and God on my
side, I have the greater advantage.

ENRICO

And if he is not?

DON JUAN

I suspect that if God was not on our side he would have

given us the larger fleet just to make his point.

Enrico and Paulo smile at this.

PAULO

May God grant you victory, admiral.

EXT. DORIA'S FRAGATA - DAY

Next day. Sunrise. As the sun crests the mountains to the east the fog lifts and burns away.

Doria stands at the bow, watching.

In the distance, behind the island, a sea of masts are visible.

As Doria watches, they begin to move. He raises the telescope and looks.

TELESCOPE POV - Two ships, Ottoman flag waving high, emerge from behind the island. Behind them, the Ottoman fleet sails into the gulf.

INT. CAPTAIN'S QUARTERS - DAY

Don Juan is again at his table. He studies charts and battle formations. He prays. Crosses himself. The door flings open. Doria stands tall in the frame.

DORIA

They are upon us. I am going to my ship. May God grant us

Victory.

DON JUAN

There is none without him.

EXT. GULF OF PATRAS - DAY

The morning sun shines bright. The sea glistens. The Holy League ships stand in formation, ready for battle.

Some distance away, the Ottoman fleet gets itself into formation.

EXT. DON JUAN'S FRAGATA - DAY

Don Juan stands amidships, splendidly arrayed, as his fragata is rowed along the flanks of the Holy League galleys.

Holy League officers and soldiers stand along the sides of their ships, listening as Don Juan speaks.

DON JUAN

By the grace of Almighty God, we have come to avenge

to atrocities you have observed at Corfu, the terrible tortures

done to his servants at Famagusta, and to rid this land and sea

of his enemies.

(MORE)

DON JUAN (CONT'D)

> Go boldly into battle, in the name of your God, and do not let these infidels taunt you. No matter the tide, no matter the turn of the sword, pay them no heed when they cry out, "Where is thy God." For he is here, among us, and he will go before us in battle.

The officers and soldiers on the ships cheer.

In the distance, a cheer is heard, followed by the rapid fire of snare drums.

Don Juan raises his telescope.

TELESCOPE POV - The Ottoman fleet is replete with men playing instruments, singing, and dancing. Some play kettle drums, some play tambourines, some play cornets.

END POV

DON JUAN (CONT'D) Dance while you can.

EXT. GULF OF PATRAS - DAY

The two fleets are in full formation, separated by some distance prior to the battle.

Revelry continues on the Ottoman ships, but is now drowned out by the same revelry on the Holy League ships.

MONTAGE:

Holy League soldiers play kettle drums, cornets, trumpets, and sackbuts.

Officers and soldiers sing battle songs and praises to God.

Don Juan dances, along with his soldiers, amidships on his fragata.

END MONTAGE

EXT. DO JUAN'S FRAGATA - DAY

Amid the pre-battle enthusiasm, Don Juan catches movement amidst the Ottoman fleet.

He motions for the music and dancing to stop. Raises his telescope.

Around him, the music stops. The silence slowly spreads along his ship, then more and more rapidly along the fleet.

Silence. Neither fleet is making music now.

TELESCOPE POV - A new flag is raised on the Ottoman flagship.

END POV

Don Juan lowers his telescope.

In the distance, a traditional Muslim call to prayer is heard.

Don Juan turns to someone behind him.

DON JUAN Make the call.

Behind him, a kettle drum and a trumpet ring out a very specific, very cadenced rhythm. The same sound is then heard from each ship in the fleet.

DON JUAN (CONT'D) To prayer!

EXT. DORIA'S FRAGATA - DAY

Doria stands amidships listening to the trumpets and kettle drums as the sound echoes down the length of the fleet.

DORIA   To

prayer!

EXT. VENIER'S FRAGATA - DAY

Venier stands at the bow, watching. The trumpet and kettle drums echo away and fade to silence.

Behind him, men stand waiting.

DeMarco approaches him.

DEMARCO

It is our call to prayer.

VENIER

The time for prayer is past. Look and see. We are out-

numbered, outgunned, and out maneuvered before we begin.

EXT. GULF OF PATRAS - DAY

MONTAGE:

On the Ottoman ships, devout soldiers bow low to the decks, facing Mecca, in sincere prayer.

On the Holy League ships, oarsmen and officers alike kneel and pray.

Don Juan kneels at the bow of his fragata, praying and clutching a rosary.

On the stern of Doria's fragata, Doria kneels while mouting a silent prayer.

END MONTAGE

EXT. VENIER'S FRAGATA - DAY

Venier and his men stand watching. Waiting.

Activity on the other ships, for both fleets, is picking up. Oarsmen, archers, and artillery get into position.

A single shot rings out from the Ottoman flagship, smoke rising from a cannon.

No impact is seen on ship or sea.

VENIER

The empty salvo. They await Don Juan's response, then the

battle will commence. At my command, turn our ships and

retreat to safety.

DEMARCO

But -

VENIER

Hear me and hear me well. If God is with Don Juan he won't

need us. And if he is not, we won't need to die.

DEMARCO

And if God is with him and grants him victory? Would you

have him honored more highly than yourself?

Venier takes this in. Before he can respond, a shot is fired from Don Juan's fragata.

The ships begin to move.

Venier wheels on his men.

> VENIER
>
> Turn and pull back!

EXT. DON JUAN'S FRAGATA - DAY

Paulo rushes to Don Juan, telescope held high.

> PAULO
>
> Admiral! Venier is retreating!

Don Juan snatches the telescope and peers through it.

TELESCOPE POV: Venier's ships are indeed turning away, creating a gap in the Holy League's defenses.

The telescope view swings left. The Ottoman ships on Venier's flank turn to pursue them.

Don Juan smiles.

> DON JUAN
>
> I don't know if he is a coward or a genius. But whatever
>
> his intent, the enemy is turning their broadside to us.

He wheels on his crew.

> DON JUAN (CONT'D) Swing full to port!
>
> Prepare a full salvo!

EXT. VENIER'S FRAGATA - DAY

Venier watches as the Ottoman vessels turn to pursue him.

> VENIER
>
> What are they doing? They should be breaching the gap we left.

A sudden roar of cannon fire explodes from Don Juan's fragata.

A moment later, one of the Ottoman ships pursuing Venier is decimated, fire and smoke billowing up, oarsmen and soldiers leaping into the sea. The ship is very close to it next ally, and swings into it's stern, causing the fire to spread between both ships.

> VENIER (CONT'D) Perhaps God is with
>
> that scoundrel after all.

He runs to the cockpit.

> VENIER (CONT'D) Turn and en-
>
> gage, and may God forgive our lack of faith!

EXT. DORIA'S FRAGATA - DAY

Doria's fragata is engaged in closer combat, and the flank of ships with him exchange fire with the Ottoman ships on their flank.

Artillerymen stand in light armor, protected by the ship's gunwales as best they can, and fire rifles at the Ottoman archers and oarsmen across the waves.

As each man fires, another rifle is handed to him. The rifle just fired is handed back to be reloaded. Each artilleryman has three rifles. One he is firing, one being handed up to him, and one being loaded.

Doria runs to the stern of his ship and calls out to his men and the captain of the ship behind him.

DORIA On my

command!

The captain of the ship behind him acknowledges his call and passes a message and a flag back to a soldier who runs astern of his own ship. A message is being carried between the ships on Doria's flanks.

Arrows from Ottoman archers rain into Doria's ship. Some miss their mark, but many find their way to the soldiers and oarsmen.

The soldiers and oarsmen wear light, arrow resistant armor, so the injuries are minor.

Rifle fire from the Ottomans sail over their heads. Some shells hit the ship. So far, none hit flesh.

Doria's artillerymen are faring about as well as the sea tosses their ships, but they are able to fire much more rapidly due to the sequence of firing and reloading they have developed.

Doria remains at the stern. Watches. Draws his ship in closer. Turns back to the captain of the ship behind him.

DORIA (CONT'D) Let fly!

EXT. OTTOMAN SHIP - DAY

OTTOMAN ARCHERS prepare their bows for another salvo when a wave of cannon fire erupts from Doria's flank.

Some of the Ottoman ships are struck, some catch fire, but many, many more are there to replace them. Doria appears to be greatly outnumbered.

Suddenly, more cannon fire erupts. Now the smoke from the fires, combined with the smoke from the cannon fire, thicken the air and obscure the archers' view, making it impossible for them to take aim.

EXT. GULF OF PATRAS - DAY

An overhead view of the battle. Enemy lines are beginning to tatter on both sides. Gaps break between the flanks.

The air is thick with smoke from cannons and from fire.

Men are seen leaping from burning ships.

Bodies are seen floating in the water.

EXT. DON JUAN'S FRAGATA - DAY

Cannon fire and rifle fire explode in a deafening roar all around.

Don Juan tries to view the battle via his telescope, but the air is too thick with smoke. He can't make out who is who.

DON JUAN

Close the ranks! Prepare to fledge and board!

EXT. VENIER'S FRAGATA - DAY

If anything, the roar of gunfire is louder here.

Venier runs up the starboard side of his fragata, shouting commands at the ships on his flank.

VENIER

Don Juan is closing ranks! Draw the enemy in and cripple

their port side!

EXT. DORIA'S FRAGATA - DAY

Doria stands at the stern, amid the roar and smoke of constant artillery.

Through the smoke he sees an Ottoman ship appear. It is badly damaged, and listing. Behind it, two more damaged ships come alongside it.

He signals to the captain of the ship immediately behind him. The captain acknowledges.

DORIA

Turn and cripple!

EXT. OTTOMAN SHIP - DAY

An Ottoman ship pulls up alongside another Ottoman ship. Both are damaged and listing.

As they attempt to tie together, a Holy League galley shoots up out of the smoke and rams their starboard side with the galley's bow, ripping a huge breach in the Ottoman vessel.

Ottoman soldiers and oarsmen tumble backwards, the oarsmen shackled to their oars by chains.

Doria's men storm the ship and begin hand to hand combat with swords, knives, and small handguns.

Doria fights among them.

One of the Ottomans wheels around with sword. Doria sees it in time to duck.

The ship lists. The Ottoman stumbles past Doria and falls into the sea.

Doria falls backwards, landing next to a SHACKLED OARSMAN.

OARSMAN

We are Greek! We are Greek!

Doria stumbles up, looks around at the other oarsmen, all shackled to their oars and staring up at him.

He fights his way through the melee and finds the ship's captain engaged in brutal combat.

The ship's captain fights well. Men fall at his side. His sword and uniform drip with blood. It is impossible to tell if any of it is his.

He sees Doria and smiles.

Doria charges and they engage. Doria looks to have the disadvantage. He stumbles back when dodging a swing of the Ottoman's sword. He falls to the ground.

The Ottoman puts a foot on his throat. Smiles. Raises his sword.

The tip of another sword plunges forward through the Ottoman's chest, then pulls back.

The Ottoman drops to the deck, dead.

Don Juan stands in his place, bloody sword in hand.

DORIA

His keys! The oarsmen are Greek!

Don Juan grabs the captain's keys.

EXT. OTTOMAN SHIP - DAY

Don Juan and Doria release the Greek oarsmen. They oarsmen grab weapons from fallen soldiers and take up the fight against their previous captors.

EXT. VENIER'S FRAGATA - DAY

An intense battle rages on Venier's fragata. He and his men fight valiantly, but there are too many ships and too many Ottomans for them to fend away.

The quarters close in, and Venier and his men are cornered.

Sudden gunfire erupts, ripping through the Ottoman attackers. Venier and his men turn to see Don Juan's artillerymen standing with smoking rifles.

The Ottoman attackers turn to fight, but they are swarmed by Greeks, who take swift and violent vengeance for their captivity.

Swords fly, blood spills. Venier and his men join in the fray.

EXT. GULF OF PATRAS - DAY

The smoke thins as the gunfire recedes. A few ships still engage, but the battle is won.

MONTAGE

Holy League sailors pull Ottoman fighters from the sea.

Ottoman prisoners are escorted to brigs.

Ottoman fighters surrender.

Ottoman ships are lashed to Holy League ships to be hauled away.

Armor and weaponry are carried off of the Ottoman ships by Holy League officers and soldiers.

END MONTAGE

EXT. DON JUAN'S FRAGATA - DAY

The sun lowers in the sky. Don Juan watches the looting of the remaining Ottoman ships.

The smoke has all but cleared, and the aftermath of the battle is laid out before him.

The Ottoman ships that remain are battered and listing, many without masts.

Many Ottoman vessels have sunk in shallow waters, their husks leaning half submerged.

Other Ottoman ships still burn out at sea.

The Holy League has suffered as well.

Holy League ships have been damaged, some beyond repair, and some have been sunk.

Bodies are carried off for internment.

All around are cheers from the survivors of his navy.

INT. CAPTAIN'S QUARTERS - DAY

Don Juan sleeps in his bed. The sun peeks through the porthole, shining a shaft of light on a thick Bible resting on his chart table.

A knock at the door.

Don Juan's eyes jerk open. He sits up.

> DON JUAN A mo-
> ment!

He stands, a little stiff, and dons his jacket. He squints out the porthole at the rising sun.

> DON JUAN (CONT'D) Come.

The door opens, revealing a ragged Doria. His face is half smile and half concern.

> DON JUAN (CONT'D) I can't tell if
> you've come to celebrate or to warn me of an im-
> pending attack.

> DORIA Perhaps both.

> DON JUAN
> What is it then? We cannot sustain another battle now.

> DORIA

It's not that kind of battle.

DON JUAN Then what?

DORIA

Have you written to the Pope and your brother?

DON JUAN Concerning?

Doria is taken aback by the question. He gestures around as if to say *all of this.*

DORIA

Of our victory, Don Juan.

DON JUAN

I felt it would be better to sail into port with the Ottoman ships in tow, carrying the papal flag on their masts. That would be a glorious statement and the glory would be God's.

DORIA

Then I'm afraid he won't be the first to gain the glory.

DON JUAN Meaning?

DORIA

Venier has already sent a letter reporting our victory, and of course the leading role he played.

Don Juan takes this in. Fumes.

DON JUAN

I'll deal with Venier.

DORIA

The damage is done, Don Juan. His will be the first news of the victory, and the most widely reported account.

Don Juan fumes a moment more, then turns and walks to his porthole. Looks out.

DON JUAN Then let it be so.

DORIA

Shall I summon Venier to you?

DON JUAN No.

DORIA

Do you intend to deal with his insolence?

DON JUAN No.

DORIA

But ... It is a great disrespect to you.

DON JUAN

Not to me. Venier once asked me if this battle was for my glory or for God's. I told him I didn't know. And until the battle commenced I didn't. But God was here, commander. He was in our midst. The glory is his.

(MORE)

DON JUAN (CONT'D)

If Venier wants to steal God's glory, let God deal with him.

Doria smiles.

DORIA

It would be more merciful for you to deal with him than
to leave to the hands of an angry God.

DON JUAN

Then perhaps I will pray for God's mercy on him.

Doria turns to go. Stops. Turns back.

DORIA

Will you? Pray for God's mercy on Venier?

Don Juan turns to face him.

DON JUAN

We should prepare the ships for the return sail. The weather
will be against us soon. We need to hasten our repairs.

EXT. DON JUAN'S FRAGATA - DAY

Don Juan stands amidships, regally dressed, addressing the troops as his fragata rows among
the vessels of the Holy League.

Soldiers and officers stand alongside the gunwales of their ships as he passes among them.

DON JUAN

By God's grace we who remain will return victorious to

our homes and families. We have fought for victory, and

God has granted it. We have lost men, and may God grant

them entry into his eternal kingdom. May you who live and

remain have the grace of Almighty God upon you from this

day forward.

INT. PALACE OF KING PHILIP II OF SPAIN - DAY

Don Juan stands looking out the window on the palace grounds.

Philip fumes, waving a paper as he speaks.

PHILIP

It was a grave error, Don Juan!

DON JUAN

It was a thing that happened.

PHILIP

And that you should have prevented! You have let Venier take
credit for the victory!

DON JUAN

> I did not let him. He simply did it without my knowledge.
> What was I to do? Execute him as soon as the battle was done
> so I could be the first to announce our victory?

PHILIP

> As soon as the battle was done, you should have dispatched
> your report while he was still licking his wounds.

Don Juan turns to face him.

> DON JUAN I am sorry, Philip. It
was an oversight on my part.
> PHILIP An oversight that may cost
us dearly.

DON JUAN

> I don't see what the problem is. This battle was for God,
> not for us.

PHILIP

> For God and profit, Don Juan. Or have you forgotten your
> own words?
> DON JUAN I've not forgotten them. I
have repented of them.

PHILIP

> I liked you better when you were less pious.

DON JUAN

> You liked me better when I was more profitable.

Don Juan walks out, leaving Philip to fume.

EXT. PALACE OF KING PHILIP II OF SPAIN - DAY Don Juan walks out of the
palace and towards the city.

Outside the gates he is met by a waiting Doria.

> DORIA How was
he?
> DON JUAN Not well.

DORIA

I suspected as much. Venier is becoming quite popular after his victory.

DON JUAN

Then let him be. He can become Doge of Venice for all it matters to me.

DORIA

You truly don't care?

DON JUAN

If it means I never have to see him again, then I am for whatever success he has.

They stand there a moment. Then:

DORIA

The Pope has his eye on Tunis.

DON JUAN

Then let him take it.

DORIA

I think, my friend, he was hoping we would take it for him.

DON JUAN

For him, or for God?

DORIA

It is the Pope, Don Juan. Not Venier.

They share a good laugh at this.

DON JUAN For God, then.

DORIA

To God be the glory.

INT. HOLY HOUSE OF LORETO - DAY

SUPER: One Year Later

Don Juan kneels in the Holy House of Loreto, before the altar, mouthing silent prayer.

Behind him enters Pope Pius V.

The Pope stands there a moment, then approaches and kneels next to Don Juan. They both pray.

INT. HOLY HOUSE OF LORETO - DAY

The light has shifted, it is much later. Pope Pius has left. Don Juan continues in his prayer.

He stops, removes his sword, and lays is on the altar.

He crosses himself. Stands. Pauses a moment. Walks out.

EXT. HOLY HOUSE OF LORETO - DAY

Don Juan and the Pope walk along the village street. The

Pope's entourage and security detail are visible everywhere.

POPE PIUS V

I wonder, Don Juan. When did you know it was God who

had won the victory?

DON JUAN

That is a difficult question. I only know that at some point

I knew. And once I did, I no longer doubted.

POPE PIUS V That is often how it goes

with faith. The moment of our belief is hard to define,

because it comes out of our obedience. As we obey, we

believe.

DON JUAN

I thought is was the other way around. We believe, and

because we believe, we obey.

POPE PIUS V

Did you believe God had chosen you for his victory when we

last spoke here?

DON JUAN No.

POPE PIUS V

And what happened to change that belief?

DON JUAN I obeyed

his call.

POPE PIUS V

Which led to your belief.

DON JUAN

Did you believe I was his choice when we last spoke here?

POPE PIUS V With all my

heart.

DON JUAN But why?

POPE PIUS V

Because you were the least likely to succeed.

A moment passes. Pope Pius looks stern. Then he smiles. They share a hearty laugh at this.

POPE PIUS V (CONT'D) It's an honor to

be the least likely, Don Juan. Think of David and Goliath.

Gideon and the Midianites. Saul on the road to Tarsus.

DON JUAN

It seems I am in good company.

POPE PIUS V

And you will continue to be, so long as you trust in God.

They approach the Pope's carriage. He steps up inside and turns back to Don Juan.

POPE PIUS V (CONT'D) I will be

praying for you, Don Juan.

DON JUAN And I for

you.

Pope Pius smiles and closes the door to his carriage. The carriage pulls away, and his entourage goes along with it.

Don Juan watches them pass by, and is left alone in the village.

A moment later he mounts his own horse and rides in the opposite direction, the sun setting behind him.

FADE OUT

WHITE TEXT OVER BLACK SCREEN

The battle of Lepanto was a decisive victory for the Holy League, and marked the reestablishment of the Christian Empire in the Levant.

Don Juan and Doria led the battle to retake Tunis from the Ottomans in 1573. The Ottomans retook Tunis in 1574 and remained in power there.

In 1576, Don Juan was appointed Governor General over the Hapsburg Netherlands. He led the capture of the city of Namur in 1577, and defeated the Protestants in the Battle of Gembloux in 1578.

After his victories, he was defeated at Rijmenam near present day Brussels. After this defeat his health began to deteriorate and he succumbed to a fever, dying on Sunday, October 1, 1578. He was 31 years old.

Doria went on to lead expeditions against the Barbary States in 1601. He also served as Commander of the Order of Santiago, the Marquis of Tursi, and Prince of Melfi.

Venier was elected Doge of Venice in 1577, at the age of 81. He died on March 3, 1578. His remains now rest at the Basilica di San Giovanni e Paulo.